AUSTRALIA
IN COLOUR

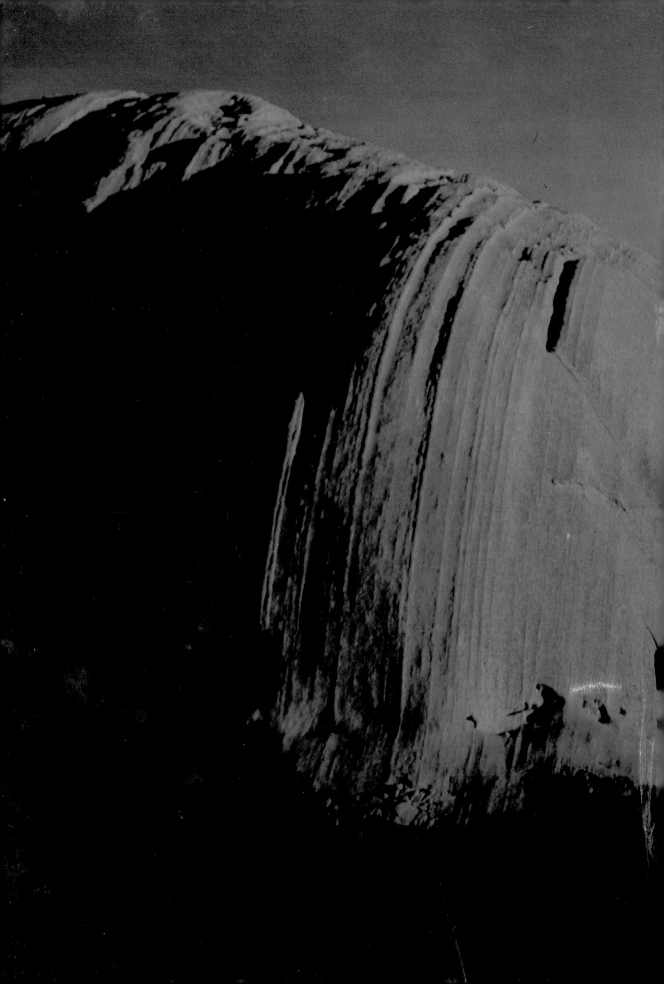

AUSTRALIA
IN COLOUR

Photographs by Fritz Prenzel

Ure Smith • Sydney

Termite mounds near Broome, Western Australia.

half title page:

The waratah is the floral emblem of New South Wales where it is mostly found.

title page: ˙
Ayers Rock is a Central Australian landmark, and is a popular tourist attraction.

First published 1976 by
Ure Smith, Sydney
a division of Paul Hamlyn Pty Ltd
1976 South Creek Road, Dee Why West, Australia 2099

Photographs © Fritz Prenzel 1976
Designed in Australia by Albert Falzon
Typeset by G.T. Setters Pty Ltd, Sydney
Printed by Dainippon Tien Wah (Pte) Limited
977 Bukit Timah Road, Singapore 21.

National Library of Australia Card Number and
ISBN 0 7254 0339 X

Chifley Square, Sydney. Photo Kurt Vollmer

Parliament House, Canberra,
reflected in the waters of Lake Burley Griffin.

Lawn bowls in the heart of Sydney.

King William Street, Adelaide, with the Town Hall.

St Mary's Cathedral, Adelaide.

Brisbane after dark.

Sydney Harbour Bridge and Opera House, looking over from Farm Cove.

Perth lies on the banks of the Swan River about 20 kilometres from its mouth at Fremantle.

Bourke Street, Melbourne, and Parliament House.

Victoria Fountain, Adelaide.

Rural scene, Victoria

Exhibition Building, Melbourne.

Brolgas are birds of the crane family. They are sometimes known as Native Companions.

The main street Rockhampton, Queensland.

Sydney Harbour, looking west from the northern beach of Manly.

Sails a-set on Sydney Harbour.

*A pandanus palm
on Queensland's Sunshine Coast.*

Surfboats are a familiar feature of the Australian lifesaving movement.

The west coast of the Tasman Peninsula, Tasmania.

Gove Peninsula in the Northern Territory has one of the world's largest deposits of bauxite.

Bell Bay, near Launceston, Tasmania, is the site of Australia's first aluminium plant.

Steelworks at Whyalla, South Australia. Photo Reg Morrison.

e 1850s, more than 20,000 miners were working the goldfields in the Victorian town of Ballarat. Today there are
reminders of the goldrush days.

Wave Rock, a granite cliff near Hyden, Western Australia. The wave-like effect has been caused by erosio.

A round-up of horses in the Northern Territory. Note the wild camels in the background. Photo Reg Morrison.

Aboriginal rock paintings at Christmas Creek in the Northern Territory. Photo Reg Morrison.

Wild buffaloes in Arnhemland, Northern Territory. These beasts were first brought into Australia in the 1820s.

Hamersley Range, Western Australia. Rich deposits of iron ore are being mined here.

Tasmania—the central plateau.

This baobab tree, in Derby, Western Australia, was once used as a prison.

One of Australia's many varieties of eucalypt.

The Three Sisters at Katoomba in the Blue Mountains west of Sydney.

Murchison River, Western Australia.

Panning for gold at Hill End, New South Wales, which was a busy goldfield in the middle of last century. Photo Kurt Vollmer.

The wombat is an Australian native animal.
It lives in burrows and feeds at night.

Adelaide from the Adelaide Hills, South Australia.

The emu is second largest of the world's birds.
It is flightless and lives only on the Australian
mainland.

Koala mother and baby. Koalas live on eucalyptus leaves and are protected in Australia.

Watering cattle near Wanganella, New South Wales.

The Barossa Valley, South Australia, the birthplace of the South Australian wine industry.

Irrigation is the lifeline for the man on the land. Photo Reg Morrison.

Australia has a viable citrus industry, Oranges comprise a major proportion of that industry.

A tobacco plantation at Bright, Victoria.

The Australian wine industry is centred mainly in South Australia where it was established by German settlers in the 1840s.

Mustering sheep near Hill End, New South Wales.

Many architectural styles exist side by side in Perth, the capital of Western Australia.

Richmond Bridge, Tasmania, was built in 1823, and is the oldest usable bridge in Australia.

An old hotel at Launceston, Tasmania's second largest city.

Apsley Gorge in the New England district, New South Wales.

The ruins of the hospital at the former penal settlement of Port Arthur, Tasmania.

The chairlift at Thredbo,
a major Australian ski resort
in the Snowy Mountains.

← CHAIRLIFT

Skiing in the Snowy Mountains.

Mount Kosciusko is the highest mountain in Australia.
It is 2228 metres high, and is in the Australian Alps.

Woodchipping near Bell Bay, Tasmania.

Mount Isa, Queensland, is an important copper and lead mining town.

Australia is a highly industrialised nation, and increasing in reliance on its own manufacture rather than imported commodities. Agricultural exports amount to more than half of Australia's total overseas trade.

The Gold Coast is a popular Australian tourist resort, stretching approximately 50 kilometres north into Queensland, from the New South Wales border.

Parliament House and Botanical Gardens, Brisbane.

When the rodeo comes to town—a social highlight.

Melbourne from the air, with the King's Domain and the Yarra River in the foreground.

An aerial view of Hobart, the capital of Tasmania.

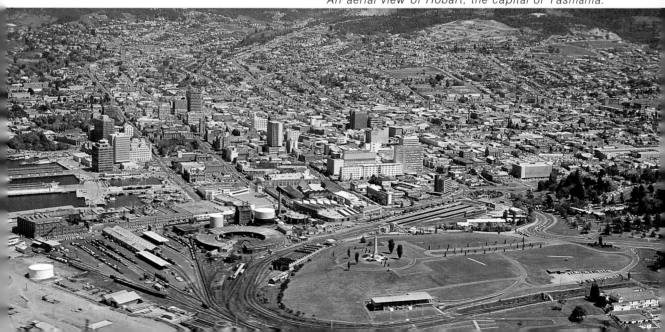

An apple plantation near Launceston, Tasmania.

Corroborees form an integral part of Australian Aboriginal lore.

Camels, first introduced to Australia in the mid-1800s as pack animals, can now be found running wild in Central Australia. Photo Reg Morrison.

Lizard Rock, Central Australia.

The Olgas, Central Australia.

The Murray River at Mildura, Victoria. In former times, the main form of transport on this river was by paddlesteamer. These are still used for tourist excursions.

Early morning at Gundagai, New South Wales.

Sugar cane harvest, Queensland.

The Ord River dam at Kununurra, Western Australia.

Floods are one of the hazards of life in rural Australia. Photo Reg Morrison.

The city of Adelaide is divided by the Torrens River, bordered by gardens and parklands.

Melbourne's colourful Moomba festival is an annual event.

ake Burley Griffin, Canberra, opposite the National
brary of Australia.

The Melbourne Cup
Australia's greatest horse-racing event.
Photo Reg Morrison.

Old tin mine, Waratah, Tasmania.

The Hunter Valley, New South Wales, noted particularly for its wine production.

The kangaroo is an exclusively Australian marsupial. With the emu, it is featured on the Australian coat of arms.

Goannas can be found throughout the Australian mainland. They grow up to 2 metres in length.

Pawpaws are a common tropical fruit found in Queensland and northern New South Wales.

A Queensland rainforest.

The Apostles, Port Campbell, South Australia. Photo Reg Morrison.

Wilson's Promontory, Victoria, is the most southerly point of the Australian mainland.

Prawning is mainly carried out in the Gulf of Carpentaria and the waters off northern Australia.

Fishing nets at Iluka, New South Wales.

Turtles are among the many marine creatures found on the Great Barrier Reef.

Australian pelicans live on fish, and are found on many inland rivers and lakes.

Green Island on the Great Barrier Reef.

Tasman Arch, near Port Arthur, Tasmania.